DO YOU WANT TO KNOW?
A Lightworker's Guide to The Universe

Cheryl Lynn

Copyright © Cheryl Lynn Ferry 2019 • All Rights Reserved.
ISBN: 978-0-578-45816-8

DEDICATION
This book is dedicated to God.

CONTENTS

Introduction:	"DO YOU WANT TO KNOW"	1
Chapter One:	YOUR EGO AND FREE WILL	3
Chapter Two:	SPIRITUAL EMPOWERMENT	7
Chapter Three:	YOU'VE GOT THE POWER	11
Chapter Four:	YOUR SPIRITUAL DREAM TEAM	17
Chapter Five:	THE TRUTHS	25
Chapter Six:	PREDICTIONS: AMERICA	31
Chapter Seven:	PREDICTIONS: THE WORLD	35
Chapter Eight:	GOD BLOCKERS	41
Chapter Nine:	MESSAGES FOR HUMANITY	45
Chapter Ten:	FUTURE VISIONS	51

Cheryl Lynn

INTRODUCTION
"DO YOU WANT TO KNOW?"

I am a Lightworker for God. My shield, armour, and sword is as mighty as all that came before me. It is my life's purpose to spread light on to humanity. To cut away the negativity that binds mankind in fear and darkness. We are living through a great time of change. An acceleration of spiritual growth to advance ourselves to a higher level. This change is unavoidable. It is a scary time in history as the veil between the spiritual levels thin to reveal the battle raging between dark and light. Humans need the tools to survive. The dark forces will have us believe that God has forgotten us. However, God has provided all of us with the ammunition we need to go boldly into this new world. This book will provide you the answers to raise up your vibrations to combat the fears that are holding you back to achieving your highest potential as a child of God.

My journey in this life was not an easy path. Like those of you reading this book, I needed clear guidance on how not to lose my footing on the physical world's obstacles. They are like tangled tree roots making you stumble. Even the most careful walkers fell from time to time. We all fall when there is no light to shine our way. God's lantern is bright. It illuminates pure love. Once God's light shines, it cannot be dimmed by anything unless you choose to dim it. Most of the time, humans do not know they are hindering their lights. They feel a longing within themselves to fill a void. Sometimes, they look for this in other humans. It never works out because you cannot expect low energy physical world "love" to replace spiritual love. Spiritual love is God's love. And only you loving yourself spiritually can bring the peace and confidence to live your truth on the earth.

This book is different than other spiritual books you may have read. It is not professionally edited. It is to stay in its raw form. There are direct messages from God and other spiritual beings. Through spirit, I was instructed not to alter it. It is to stay as it is. I was also told strongly by spirit that there has never been anything created by humans that everybody approved of. Not one piece of art, not one book. I was to write this book without any intention to people please.

Do You Want To Know?

Just write it. God would provide the beautiful souls to read it. You are one of those beautiful souls God has chosen.

You will get positive results in your life if you follow the information. This is a good reference book to keep when you need God's guidance on situations you may face. It is also part of my Lightworker's purpose to provide future predictions. Some call it the gift of prophecy. I use my gift to see into the future to give clarity to others. To give them the information they need to make the best decisions they can for their futures. It also helps to calm fears to know when something is going to happen and you can prepare for it.

It is an honor for me to serve God. To be a part of everything. I am blessed by the thousands of people that have listened to my videos. I am blessed by my clients that I have had the honor to do readings for throughout the years. I am blessed by my family here on earth. I am blessed by the countless spiritual beings that are with me and helping me as I walk my path.

Find the love and joy in your life as I found mine. Know the real God not the world's God. Most importantly, love yourself. When you love yourself, you love God.

DO YOU WANT TO KNOW?

Turn the pages and begin your journey.

God loves you. So do I.

Cheryl Lynn, Lightworker

CHAPTER ONE
YOUR EGO AND FREE WILL

Whether it is spirituality or any paths to God, I expect miracles to happen. I expect God and the angels to come through for me. To be there always. Every moment, every second of my time here on earth. Loving, guiding, and protecting me as I live my truth. Helping me always and in all ways.

You are reading this book because you want miracles to happen for you, too. God loves us all the same. God and our Higher Self wants us to live our truths to the highest levels. To be a blessing to ourselves and the world. Nothing is impossible with God in control. It is important that you speak your truth and live your truth as I have outlined in this book. To surrender total control to God. After you do that, there are two obstacles that you must overcome to see results. Once you overcome these two obstacles, miracles happen.

The two obstacles I speak of is your ego and free will. Separately or together, they block the miracles and good in your life. And yes, they even block God. That is why it is so important you have the information about your ego and free will.

EGO. THE DEVIL IN YOUR HEAD.

It lies to you. It thrives on fear and guilt. It is one of the lowest and most negative energies on earth. It pulls you down and keeps you down. It is where nightmares thrive. It loves to keep reminding you of the past. All the regrets, all the sorrows. It tells you God hates you. You are not good enough for Him or anything. It creates anxiety and worry to distract you from your life's purpose.

I am being a little dramatic here but I want to prove my point. Your ego is great for survival. It kicks in when you are hungry or thirsty or cold. Other than that, it is a blockage. You must overcome your ego. You must raise up your vibrations past it so that the Universe can help you.

Do You Want To Know?

Fear is the food of ego. Your ego wants you in fear. To live in your ego is to live in fear. Worry and anxiety is fear of a future event that has not happened yet. You cannot live your truth and be in fear. Guilt is one of the lowest, negative energies on earth. You feel the most separated from God when you are feeling guilty. But fear and guilt can be eliminated from your life. You can live above your ego.

Once you experience the freedom of being above your ego, you never want to go back to it. So, how do you overcome this low energy entity that has been with you since birth? How can you rise above all the fear and lies that are in your head all the time? The answer is Archangel Michael. He is a mighty warrior angel with a big sword that can cut away all the negativity and raise up your vibration. He works quickly and gets the job done!

He is waiting right now for you to call on him so he can go to work. What you need to do is say, "Archangel Michael, I call upon you now to come in and cut away all the negativity energy and my fear based ego with your mighty sword. I give you permission to override my free will for my highest and greatest good. Come in and raise up my vibrations passed my ego so I may live in peace. Thank you, Archangel Michael."

That is all you need to do. No fancy prayers. Just ask for his help. You never bother him as he (and all the angels) are able to be with everyone at the same time.

If you find yourself slipping back into negative self-talk, simply repeat the prayer to Archangel Michael. He will come in as before. Start training your thoughts and speech to be positive. Remember that you create your own reality. What you think and what you speak will manifest in your life. So, keep it positive!

FREE WILL. LET IT GO TO LET THEM IN.

I must admit, when I discovered I had to let go of my free will in order for spiritual beings to come in and change my life, I was creeped out. I had visions of flying demons taking over my soul forcing me to do their evil bidding. I know that with God and the angels in charge, I am safe from that. Still, I had The Exorcist's theme song playing in my head.

Cheryl Lynn

Our free will is a gift from God. It allows us to live our life on our terms without interference from the Universe. We are free to experience all the problems, obstacles, depressions, and stresses we choose to experience for ourselves. Good and difficult. Even God respects our free will.

We must give the archangels, angels, spirit guides, guardian angels, ascended masters, saints, and God our permission to override our free will for our highest and greatest good. To come in and take over. Co-captaining our ship with God and our higher self. To release control from our ego and do it God's way.

Once you give them permission to override your free will for your highest and greatest good, they immediately come in and spring to action! You have opened the door for them to help you and get you on your path of living your truth. You will find yourself changing for the better. Your prayers have more power and meaning. You see yourself and others through God's vision of pure love.

It is also a great act of faith to release your free will to God. For you are surrendering and releasing all expectations and perfectionism on how your truths will play out. You will rely heavily on divine timing and God's perfect plan for you. Remove these obstacles in your life path today and watch the miracles God brings to you!

CHAPTER TWO
SPIRITUAL EMPOWERMENT

You are not living to your full potential. You have compromised yourself and your dreams because of others. You have allowed fear and your ego to lie to you about how you should live your life. You have felt guilty if you try to put yourself first.

And even if you attempt to live differently, you will fail. You will be poor. You will be alone. God will hate you. You don't have the time to pursue your true path as you are working hard and barely fitting in everything you need to do in a day.

Sound familiar? Excuse after excuse on why you are not living your truth. The reason you are here, the reason you were created. Your life's purpose shoved so deeply inside of yourself. Your fear (ego) keeping guard over it. Locked up tight. Well, it is time to free the prisoner!

Through Spiritual Empowerment, you can live your truth. You can wake up each day and feel truly happy knowing you are doing exactly what you were meant to do. Putting your faith and trust in God instead of the ego. God will never let you down. Once you put God in charge, everything will make sense and fall into place for you.

Here are the steps for you to follow to find Spiritual Empowerment:

TELL YOUR TRUTH TO GOD.

It is important that you are very honest with yourself when you speak your truth. Find a quiet and private place where you will not be interrupted. Close your eyes and relax. When you are ready, open your eyes and say out loud "God, I am ready to speak my truth". You need not worry that God will judge you on whatever you say. God loves you. At this point, start talking to God. Tell God what you truly would love to do with your life. Do not hold yourself back. Do not fear.

Do You Want To Know?

Just keep talking to God. Tell God all your worries. Give to God all your emotional burdens and obstacles that hold you back from living your truth. Give it all to God. After you have spoken your truth, you must give God your permission to override your free will for your highest and greatest good. Once you do this, God is in charge. You step away from it and let God handle it. You are no longer in control of your truth, God is.

START LIVING YOUR TRUTH, DO SOMETHING EVERYDAY TOWARDS YOUR TRUTH.

Once you discover what you truly would love to do with your life, you must do something every day towards your truth. This could include reading books or taking classes about your truth. Volunteering in a place related to your truth. If your truth involves opening a shop, you might start looking at store front properties to rent in your area. If your truth is to work with animals, you might help out with a local dog rescue group or be involved with fundraisers related to animals. Whatever your truth is, do something. Do not worry about the extra time or expense. Give these concerns to God. You will be provided for as you work on your truth.

LET GO, LET GOD. GOD TAKES CARE OF THE WHEN AND HOW.

Once you give your truth to God, do not worry about when it will happen or how it will happen. God is in charge. God will bring about the perfect timing for you. If you put specific time limits and how you want your truth to play out, you have allowed your ego to come in. The ego destroys, it does not accomplish anything. Keep God in control at all times. No expectations, no perfectionism.

ASK THE ANGELS TO RAISE UP YOUR VIBRATIONS TO GO PAST YOUR EGO.

The ego is a negative, low vibration entity in your head. It pulls your energy down. It lies to you. In order for you to live your truth, you must get your ego out of the way. That is where the angels come in! Those wondrous creations from God have the power to cut away all the negativity from your ego and to raise up your vibrations past it. Once you overcome your ego and function at a higher level, all things are possible. You will no longer live in fear. You will no longer believe the lies the ego tells you. You will come to know that you control your destiny and outcome, not your ego. Archangel Michael can do this for you. Call upon him to help you cut away all the negativity in your life and to raise up your vibrations. Archangel Michael is a huge angel with a large sword. He gets things done quickly. You must give Archangel Michael permission to override your free will for your highest and greatest good. Once you do this, he goes to work! You will feel lighter. Hope is restored. When you feel yourself being pulled down and your ego starts talking to you, call upon Archangel Michael to help you. He will never let you down.

STAY IN THE NOW, MOVE ON FROM THE PAST.

Once you speak your truth to God, it is important you live in the present. Do not allow your ego to keep pulling you back to the past. Keep in the NOW. The ego loves to gain control by keeping you in the past and rehashing all the guilt and pain you most likely felt. Let it go. God is in charge. Keep moving forward, living each day in God's love and protection. Find your joy in the NOW. None of us is guaranteed to live one moment longer. Cherish the time to live your life's purpose fully. With God, there is nothing to hinder you but you. Let go of your past, enjoy the present, and let God take care of your future. Yes, it is that simple!

EMPOWER YOURSELF WITH GOD.

    Spiritual Empowerment will change you. You will come to know how powerful you truly are as a spirit and part of the human experience. You will love yourself as God loves you. You will see others with different eyes because you now have God's vision, which sees only love and truth. Miracles happen daily as the angels make their presence known through signs and messages. You are assured you are never alone. You live your life's purpose without fear. You make a difference in this world. Through God, you find peace of mind, peace of heart, and peace of soul. And that is what we all want. God is waiting for you to speak your truth.

Cheryl Lynn

CHAPTER THREE
YOU'VE GOT THE POWER!

One of my favorite movie scenes is from "The Wizard of Oz". It is near the end of the film. Dorothy had completed her journey in Oz. She could go no further. All of her friends got what they were searching for but her. She wanted to go home.

There was no more moving forward on the yellow brick road, she could only turn back. She could live a life in Oz with her friends and dog but she knew that was not the right path for her. She wanted to go home.

Fortunately, Glinda the good witch appeared. There was a great sigh of relief because everybody knew Glinda could grant Dorothy her wish and send her home. The surprising twist was that Dorothy had the power all along throughout her journey in Oz to go home. She had the power all along. Once Dorothy discovered she controlled her destiny, she clicked her heels three times and went home.

We are very much like Dorothy. We have had the power all along. We may not wear magic ruby slippers to get us where we need to go but we control our path as Dorothy controlled hers.

We choose the quality of our life. Every obstacle or negative experience is created by us. God desires us to be happy and healthy. To live our lives productively and with joy. It is our ego, self-talk, and thoughts that hinder our full potential. We stand in our own way. We block the flow of prosperity. We built the obstacle walls we try to climb over. We attract the wrong people in our life. We choose everything we experience on earth.

I know it is hard to believe. I was skeptical, too. How could I choose such a horrible childhood and emotionally abusive parents? How could I live my entire young adulthood in an emotional, self-hatred prison? Why would I choose to live in personal poverty as others advanced their careers and financial freedoms?

It is our low negative energy, lying ego that tells us to do these things. To stay in despair and guilt. To keep thinking negative thoughts. The ego does not want us to know the truth about our personal power. That we can overcome the lies it tells us. It keeps us in fear and fear-based thinking. We choose fear because that is all we know. That is why it is so important for all of us to rise above our egos.

Once I discovered the secret of living above my ego, my life changed! I no longer live my life in fear. I choose to see myself as God sees me. I experience miracles from the universe every day. I take responsibility for my own personal happiness, I do not rely on others for happiness. I am living my life's purpose to the fullest and I find joy in myself and others.

It is very easy to defeat your ego and raise up your vibrations. I have written about this already but I want to say it again because it is the key to true happiness. The first thing you need to do is call upon Archangel Michael to come in and cut away your ego. To raise up your vibrations passed your ego and change your life. That you no longer believe the lies your ego tells you. You want to live your life in joy not fear. To cut away all the guilt and cords that bind you to the earth. You MUST give him permission to override your free will for your highest and greatest good. Once you do that, Archangel Michael goes to work!

Anytime you feel your vibrations going lower and your ego chimes in, call upon Archangel Michael to raise up your vibrations again. He always will. He will never not come through for you. You can call on him for anything. It does not matter if it is a big or small issue. You never bother him or the rest of the beautiful spiritual beings helping you. They will never let you down.

Here are some truths that we all need to know about us:

YOU CREATE YOUR OWN REALITY. THOUGHTS ARE THINGS.

YOU are creating your reality right now. You are the only one choosing the day by day, moment by moment life you are experiencing. Are you happy? Do you feel fulfilled and at peace with yourself and the situation? If so, then keep going. You are making the right choices for you.

If not, then you must make a change. We are all here on earth to live out our life's purpose. The true reason why we are here. When we veer off the course of our life's purpose, many things can happen to stop us from getting too far away from it. Some people experience depression or a feeling of hopelessness. Other people become angry and medicate themselves with drugs or alcohol. Some experience the 'merry-go-round' effect. This is where you keep going through the problems over and over and over again.

God and rest of the Universe will not change these things for you. That was a shocker to me when I found that out. We are in control as long as our free will is calling the shots. No spiritual being including God will override your free will and help until you tell them to. I understand some people want to experience life totally through their free will. That is, of course, their free will.

I must say when I found out that my free will was blocking the help from the universe that I needed, I gave them all permission to override my free will immediately. Once I did that, my life changed instantly for the better!

Your thoughts have much power. You manifest things in your life through your thoughts and what you verbally say. If you speak and think negative things, that is what you create. You get into habits with words and behaviors. It is very important that you think and speak positively.

This will take some practice. Words like "you kill me" or "kill two birds with one stone" or "I hate…" are negative. Most people say these words without realizing the impact they have on themselves and others. You will manifest what you think and say. Be very conscientious of what goes through your head and out of your mouth. Keep it positive!

THERE IS NO SUCH THING AS SCARCITY. IT IS AN ILLUSION.

God created abundance. There is plenty for everybody. He wants us happy, healthy, and prosperous. We block our prosperity through fear. Our ego tells us that there is not enough to go around. We will be poor and living on the streets. We do not deserve to be happy.

Do You Want To Know?

We have to aggressively push ourselves and take what crumbs we can get from life. No matter how hard we try, we always end up a day late and a dollar short.

I had this mindset for a good majority of my younger life. I was angry that everybody else made a decent living from their work but me. My employment consisted of part time, minimum wage retail jobs. I had to rely on my parents and then my husband to pay my bills. It was humiliating for me.

I created this reality for myself. I lived my life totally in my ego and fear based thinking. I believed I did not deserve to be happy and prosperous, so I was not. It was when I got out of my ego and relied on God for my success that things turned around for me.

The secret is to live your truth. Once you do that, the way is much easier. You prosper by pursing your life's purpose. It is never too late to turn your financial situation around. Once you see God's true blessings flowing into your life, you will never want to go back.

You cannot change anybody's free will. You only have power over your own.

God created free will. It is a powerful thing. Our free will allows us to live our life on our own terms without interference from the Universe. We can make our own mistakes without any spiritual intervention to fix those mistakes.

So many times, we want somebody to change for us. How many times have you said to yourself that you can change somebody into the person you want them to be? It never works, does it? The only person you can change is yourself. We can never override someone else's free will. It does not matter how much effort you put into the person, their free will remains the same.

I was someone who thought I could change others. I put in years of work hoping they would change into who I thought they should be. And when it was all finished, they stayed the same. Their free will was stronger than ever. I have so many clients asking me when somebody they love will change and become the boyfriend/spouse/parent they need them to be. I must tell them that the best they can do is pray for them and find the love they crave within themselves.

Prayer is a powerful thing. It cannot change other's free will but it can bring about miracles in their lives to want to change. Do not be frustrated if others do not want to change. If God cannot override their free will, neither can we.

We all have the same guaranteed playing field. What the greatest people in history had, we have too. It is up to us to use it.

No matter what we are born into in this world, we have the same spiritual power as the greatest of human beings. We have the same access to spiritual help. God loves us all the same. It is up to us to tap into our true selves.

Think of it, we have the same power as Abraham Lincoln. We are just as blessed as Mother Mary and Jesus. We have the chance to change the world like Dr. Martin Luther King Jr. or Gandhi. We can tap into our boundless imaginations like Walt Disney or Thomas Edison. These wonderful people started out the same as us.

The one thing they and the millions of other "special" people have in common is that they trusted in God to guide their life paths. Our ego and fear based thinking block us from our full potential. That is why it is very important you figure out your life's purpose and move forward with God leading the way.

You are your biggest obstacle to greatness. Once you find your life's passion, move on it right away! Do not listen to your doubting ego that will give you a million lies why you cannot do it. Trust in God and walk your path without fear.

I am so grateful that Lincoln and the rest of our positive changers of the world did this. You have no excuse. Start using your power now!

CHAPTER FOUR
YOUR SPIRITUAL DREAM TEAM

We are never alone. It does not matter if you live in total isolation with no human contact, you are not alone. You have an awesome spiritual dream team that surrounds you. Loving you and waiting on you to call on them for anything. They have been with you since you were created and will stay with you for eternity.

For the most part, your ego and free will blocks them from you. They will not override your free will if you do not give them permission to do so. The low energy fear-based ego in your head tells you lies. It tells you they are not real and even if they are real, they will not help you. They have other things to do more important then you and your life. This is not true. Far from being true, yet most people believe their egos. What is true is that you must give your spiritual dream team permission to override your free will for your highest and greatest good. Release your free will so they can come in and do their awesome stuff! And trust me, they work quick. Then, get your self-doubting ego out of the way. Raise up your vibration to their level. You do this through Archangel Michael. I gave you the information on how to do this in the "Your Ego and Free Will" Chapter.

Once the blockages are removed, watch your spiritual dream team go to work! Results, miracles, and positive change is what I experienced with my dream team and so will you. Call on them for anything. Nothing is too small or inconvenient for them. You are not pulling them away from bigger world issues because they can be everywhere at all times.

Here is a list of your spiritual dream team players:

GOD

Who else could I put first but our loving creator? And I mean loving. Please do not fear God. Do not listen to the man-made fear-based lies about a mean and vengeful God. Our creator is love, that is it. God is neither male nor female. God is in every molecule, every person. God does not view us in our living bodies, He views us as our true selves in spirit. He sees only love. I have found that God is the easiest energy to connect with. His energy is different for everybody. His greatness and power is beyond any words. How awesome it is that He is always there with us at every moment just waiting for us to talk to Him? I know when I connect to God's energy, it is an overwhelming feeling of love. I end up crying from all the love I feel. No other energy brings in this kind of emotion for me. There is no negativity or judgements from God. We bring on the negativity and judgements to ourselves.

How wonderful would the world be if we saw each other as God sees us. We are already perfect for God, there is no need for perfectionism in our life. We are perfect. There is no lake of fire or hell He will send you to. You create that kind of reality for yourself, not God. He is ready to help you, all you need to do is ask. No fancy prayers, just talk to Him.

HIGHER SELF

You have heard the term 'a chip off of the old block'. Well, you are the chip and your higher self is the block. Like all things, your higher self was created by God.

Your higher self is a spark of pure love from God. There are an infinite number of these lights in the universe. You are an extension off of your higher self. Extending out from your higher self is many lifetimes. Past, present, and future. These lifetimes are all happening at the same time. And yes, there are several lifetimes going on in the present, which you are a part of.

We all experience being male and female. We all experience living on other planets. We all experience death at different ages and by different ways. Time as we know it does not exist in the universe. So, it most certainly is possible for everything to be happening at once. Lineal time measurement is an earth/human thing. Since the human body is animal based, it is meant to measure the deterioration of the body.

Our higher self and God are our co-creators for this lifetime and all our lifetimes. When you meditate, you can clearly hear your higher self. It is always positive, direct, and in your own voice.

ARCHANGELS

Archangels are the work horses in the angelic realm. Created by God, they get the job done. When you have a problem in your life that you call out to God for help, He sends the archangels. Mother Mary is in charge of these angels. She is like a heavenly dispatcher making sure the proper archangel is sent to the correct person/situation.

Each archangel has a specific job to do. The most popular among these angels is Michael. He is a huge archangel with a giant sword. He can cut away all negativity in your life and defeat your fear-based ego thinking patterns. He has a mighty shield that can protect you from dark entities. He is the master of all forms of protection. There is nothing or no one who can defeat this miraculous warrior angel. He is with me constantly. I rely on his strength and protection at all times. The miracles Michael has performed in my life is countless. I am grateful for him. I walk down my path in life with him right by my side.

For health or healing issues, we have the ultimate physician in Archangel Raphael. He works on all forms of health. This includes the maintenance of a healthy body. He wants all of us to eat properly and get plenty of exercise. He has an awesome green light that he surrounds us with as his energy comes in. This green light is for all health issues and healing. He works closely with human doctors as well. He prefers organic foods and fresh water as our main diet. He leads us to natural medicines and herbal teas to help the delicate human body heal itself. You cannot miss Raphael's energy when he is around. It is strong and direct.

Archangel Gabriel is the messenger. He is in charge of all forms of communication. He is around me right now as I write this book. He is also a lot of fun and wants all of us to find more joy in our lives. He was the angel in the Bible that proclaimed to Mary about the special, beautiful child she was carrying. Sometimes his energy can be feminine or softer than the other archangels. When he delivers a message, he will make some kind of noise for us to pay attention to our intuition or signs. For me, I usually hear a police or ambulance siren. He will deliver messages to all of us differently.

There are so many archangels that do so many things. Archangel Uriel is the bringer of light from darkness. Archangel Ariel represents the outdoors and feminine strength. Archangel Metatron is all about geometry, children, and the evolution of humankind. There are countless books written on these wonderful angels and what they do. Whether we know their name or not, they come in to help. They do not want to be worshipped, however, they do want to be thanked. I am grateful every day for them.

ANGELS

There are an infinite number of angels in the universe. All of them created by God. They surround us at every moment. There are angels of romance, the home, joy, the outdoors, health, exercise, ocean, childhood, trauma, protection, etc. The list is endless. You know when an angel is near as they leave signs to reassure us that we are never alone. When you ask the Universe to "give you a sign", it is an angel that does it. Some signs from angels is finding coins everywhere, seeing rainbows or the word rainbow, clouds forming pictures, birds, the word angel, and finding feathers. They are with us always and they want us to pay attention to their signs.

You have power over your angels. You can send a million of your angels to help out a sick friend or a person in need. You can surround yourself with millions of angels for protection (that is what I do). They are happy to help because that is why they are there. Like the archangels, they do not want to be worshipped, just acknowledged for their presence in your life.

SPIRIT GUIDES

We all have a purpose in our life. A destiny we created for our self on The Other Side to fulfill here on earth. We choose spirit guides to help us stay on track. These spiritual beings must have lived at least one lifetime here on earth so they can understand the human condition and the human ego. They go through special training on The Other

Side to become guides. It is their job to stay with us as we walk our path, to keep us moving forward.

There is at least one main guide and several background guides with us at all times. They do have names and if you discover their names, please use it when you talk to them. It makes it more personal for you and them. Our deceased family members, friends, and pets can become our guides, too. They go through the same training as our main spirit guides. They are not the guides that come with us as we start our life path but they join in along the way if they choose to. The more the merry, I say.

I have found spirit guides to be very direct. They help me when I am doing readings for others. They provide me with clear visions and answers. For me, it is always a very strong message I am to deliver to my clients or myself. Just like all spiritual beings, they cannot override your free will. Give them permission to come in and give you clear, strong guidance as you walk your path.

GUARDIAN ANGELS

We are all lucky to get two of these special angels when we enter this earth and they stick with us even after we depart. Just as their name suggests, they guard and protect us. They never leave us. Many children see their guardian angels. Sometimes, these angels are mistakenly called "imaginary friends" by the children's parents.

I remember very clearly my guardian angels as a young child. They were loving and playful. They kept telling me that everything would be alright.

One guardian angel is the nurturer and the other one is more action oriented. When you feel an intense hug or wave of love flowing over you, that is your nurturing angel. Your action oriented angel gently nudges you to get going on your life's purpose. They also remind you to start that diet or stop smoking, etc.

They do have names. You can get their names through meditation. Just like all spiritual beings they have no gender, however, they can come across as masculine or feminine energy. My guardian angel names are Stephan and Raguel. They keep a close watch over me and I am thankful for them. Your guardian angels do the same for you.

ASCENDED MASTERS AND SAINTS

Ascended masters are people that lived extraordinary lives on earth. They have chosen to help out humankind with their miraculous gifts. There are many ascended masters around us at any given time. They come in when they are called or needed.

One of the most popular ascended masters is Jesus Christ. He is loved and celebrated around the world. His love and miracles for us is never ending.

Another popular and powerful ascended master is Mother Mary. You do not need to be catholic to call on her. She is in charge of the archangels. She also helps to empower women and children. Just like her son, she is a miracle worker. Her energy is very loving and nurturing. For those of us that do not have a proper mother figure in our life, Mother Mary provides that motherly love.

Buddha (who is slim in appearance, by the way), Quan Yin, Gandhi, Mary Magdalene, Confucius, and Moses are a few other ascended masters. There are so many from so many time periods. Male and female. All races and countries. Each one has a different gift to offer us. I feel their love surrounding me at all times.

Along with these wondrous ascended masters we have on our spiritual dream team is the saints. Again, you do not need to be catholic to tap into the saints loving energy. A popular saint is Francis. He is well known for his loving care of animals. Saint Nicholas' giving spirit is felt around the Christmas holiday, however, you can tap into this energy all year long. I call upon Saint Theresa every time I travel to keep me safe. Saint Anthony is the finder of lost things. This could be anything from finding your keys to finding a lost child.

Just like the ascended masters, there are too many saints to mention in this book and what they do. They are all ready to help us, all we need to do is ask.

Cheryl Lynn

We all have this spiritual dream team with us. Nothing is too big or too small for our spiritual dream team to accomplish. All we need to do is give them permission to override our free will for our highest and greatest good. Let them come in and perform miracles in your life as they have done in mine.

They love you unconditionally. Put your spiritual dream team in play today!

CHAPTER FIVE
THE TRUTHS

    I was the biggest skeptic when it came to living your truth. I am a results person. Pretty words and loving God is wonderful but if it did not change my life, what is the point? I was not interested if miracles did not happen. I had enough let downs in my life. I did not want God letting me down, too. Through faith, I walked down the path of Spiritual Empowerment. I was uncomfortable at first because I had to let go of all control in my life and put it in God's hands.

    I said to myself that I will give this a try. I will live these "Truths". The angels assured me I was loved and protected every step I took. I started this journey with God. Deep within me I knew I would not stick with it if I did not see a total change in my life and in me. God did not disappoint me. My life changed right away. I want to give you these "Truths". They work.

LIVE IN INTEGRITY. SPEND YOUR TIME DOING ACTIVITIES THAT MATCH YOUR HIGHEST INTENTIONS. LET GO OF THE REST.

    Live your truth every day. Devote your time to pursuing your truth. Release ALL things and activities that take you away from your truth. They are a distraction. Give all your concerns to God as you walk your daily path.

THERE IS ONLY NOW.

    Stay in the present because that is what you truly have. It is fine to look back to the past for life lessons you learned, however, do not dwell in the past. Your ego loves to keep you trapped in the past, especially if you feel guilty about something. Give your past to God. Stay in the now. You are not guaranteed to live one moment longer.

Do You Want To Know?

God will direct your future, release any expectations on it. Live in the now and focus your energy on it.

ALL CONFLICT IS INSIDE YOUR MIND. ANY CONFLICT YOU EXPERIENCE IS THE PROJECTION FROM YOUR EGO.

You create your own reality. If there is hardship and conflicts in your life, you have created them. You have allowed your negative, lower energy ego to control your life. Once you give your reality over to God and living your truth, the ego cannot compete. The only way the ego has any say is if you give it the power to do so. Fortunately, there are countless loving spiritual beings surrounding you to help you stay on track and out of conflict. Give them permission to override your free will for your highest and greatest good and watch them work!

PURIFY YOUR DIET. ELIMINATE ALL TOXINS. THIS INCLUDES MEAT, SUGAR, CAFFEINE, ALCOHOL, DAIRY, AND CHOCOLATE. DO AN ORGANIC FRESH FRUITS AND VEGGIES DIET. INCLUDE NON-ANIMAL PROTEINS.

We human beings were not meant to digest all these toxic chemicals that are in our foods today. Our bodies deteriorate quickly. They need the proper nutrition to function at their peak. You want to have plenty of time and health to live out your truth, that is why you must change your eating habits. Switch over to organic foods. Eat plenty of fruits and vegetables. Eliminate dairy products and embrace non-dairy based yogurts and cheeses. If you must eat meat, stick with fresh fish and organic free range chicken. Use organic ground turkey meat instead of ground beef. Stop drinking soda immediately! Limit your coffee intake. If you drink coffee, make sure it is organic. Water, water, water! Drink plenty of water. It is so important you feed yourself properly. Please know that God and the angels will help you all along the way as you change your diet. It will not happen overnight. Little by little and eventually you will be eating correctly.

DO NOT GIVE IN ORDER TO GET SOMETHING BACK IN RETURN. JUST GIVE AND LET GOD DO THE REST.

If you want to extend a courtesy to someone then just do it. Do not have the mindset that if you give you will get back. If you want to donate your money to someone or a charity, then just do it and let it go. Do not give your money because you expect God to give you an increased payback. Just give and leave the rest to God. You will be blessed in God's way and in God's time.

SPEND TIME ALONE IN NATURE.

It is important for all of us to spend time alone in nature. No distractions. Get outside and breathe the fresh air. Our bodies need sunshine. It is also an excellent way for the angels to clear our minds from all the toxins and negativity it absorbs. Meditation is very important to receive messages from the angels, God, and our higher self. Sitting quietly in nature is a form of meditation. If you can, get away to a beach or mountain retreat to recharge your spiritual batteries and refresh yourself. Taking a walk outside every day costs nothing but helps rejuvenate our minds and bodies. Get outside!

DETACH FROM MATTER. DO NOT PUT YOUR FOCUS ON MATERIAL THINGS. PUTTING YOUR FOCUS ON MATERIAL THINGS ONLY LOWERS YOUR ENERGY INTO YOUR FEAR-BASED EGO. GOD KNOWS WHAT YOU NEED.

Scarcity is an illusion. There is plenty for everybody. There are unlimited financial and material resources for us all. When you start living your truth and putting your full focus on your truth, you will be provided for materially by God. We create our own reality. If you are working a stressful job and trying to make ends meet without results, you are creating that reality for yourself. Your ego loves to keep you on that hamster wheel of debt. When you live your truth, there is no stress. Things fall into place because God is in charge.

JUDGE NOT. WE ARE NOT HERE TO JUDGE EACH OTHER. WE ARE HERE TO LOVE AND SUPPORT EACH OTHER.

It is all about love. God is love. The angels are love. And yes, we are spirits made out of love from God. That's it in a nutshell, folks. With all the complexities in the Universe, it all boils down to love. God loves us all and He created everything because of love. When God looks at us, He sees only the spiritual love being He created. He does not see color of skin or sexual preference. He does not see physical deformities. He does not see a person's weight or height. He does not see culture or religion. He does not see poverty or great riches. He sees us as we truly are. We are here to help each other. To see others as God sees us. When you live your truth, it always has a helpful component to it. It is always for the greater good in yourself and others. In other words, living your truth is love.

YOU LIVE WHERE YOUR CONSCIOUSNESS IS FOCUSED. THOUGHTS ARE THINGS. YOUR THOUGHTS ARE VERY POWERFUL. NEGATIVE THOUGHT PATTERNS PRODUCE NEGATIVITY. TRAIN YOUR THOUGHTS TO STAY POSITIVE.

Oh, how your ego loves to control you through your thoughts! Whatever you think will materialize. If you think negative things about yourself and others, negative things will happen. If worry, guilt, and anxiety fill your head, that is what will be in your life. A ton of worry, guilt, and anxiety. It is very important you overcome your ego and its negative thought patterns. Ego's food is fear. Through fear, the ego keeps you and your thoughts in low energy negativity. Anxiety and worry is fear of a future event that has not happened yet. If you would stay in the NOW, there would not be worry or anxiety. Guilt is the lowest of energies. The ego loves for us to feel guilty. If it can get you to stay in the past and keep reliving the guilt you felt, all the better. That is why it is very important to raise your vibration up past your ego. Once you do that, your thoughts will turn positive and change can happen. The way you raise up your vibration is to call upon Archangel Michael. He has a mighty sword that can cut away the negativity and protect you from your ego. Give Archangel Michael permission to override your free will for your highest and greatest good. Once you do that, he will go to work! You will feel at peace in your mind as he takes you out of your ego. Once this happens, train yourself to think only positive thoughts. Do not lower your energy again into the ego. Keep in the NOW and keep in the positive. After some time, you will learn to stay in the positive. If you feel yourself going back into the negative, call upon Archangel Michael to cut away the negativity and to raise up your vibration. Archangel Michael will never let you down.

GIVE GLORY TO GOD IN ALL THINGS. IT IS NOT ABOUT US, IT IS ABOUT GOD. SEEK NOT SELF PRAISE OR GLORY. WHEN WE GIVE GOD THE GLORY, WE GLORIFY THE SPARK OF GOD THAT IS WITHIN OURSELVES.

Give it ALL to God. Everything. When we put God first in our life and give Him total control over our life, it works. The roadblocks disappear as we live our truth and see others as God sees them. Self-praise and fame are negative. It is very difficult to live a spiritual life and be famous. They are two opposing energies. Giving God all the glory opens the door for God to work to your highest and greatest good. Give God all the praise and all the pain. You can always trust God.

CHAPTER SIX
PREDICTIONS: AMERICA

America will never be the same again. It is evolving and turning into something different then what most of us think America should be. These changes are not to be feared for without them, humanity is gone. The rapid advancements in technology is bringing about these changes much quicker than most people are ready for.

I will tell you my vivid visions for America. I will hold nothing back. I do not have a specific timeline for my visions, only that they will happen.

America and its people will be cut down to the root in order for a new tree to grow. It will be a stronger tree.

I had a strong vision of an old twisted tree. There were many branches on the tree but they were dying. The tree had weathered many storms and the roots could no longer support the decaying tree. It could no longer bear fruit. It was suffering from being dead within the trunk. It needed to be cut down and it was. I saw many people weeping over the loss of the tree.

A new tree was planted with stronger roots.

MY VISIONS FOR AMERICA.

First of all, humans themselves change in appearance. They are taller with bigger feet. A noticeable body structure change. Their digestive systems are different as they cannot tolerate the chemicals in the food. They mostly eat organic fruits and vegetables.

I see America's east and west coast chewed up. The water is coming. I do not see Miami, the Florida Keys, or the Jersey Shore. The water levels will rise. I see the Maryland Shores gone. Major flooding in New York City. People leaving the city because of the flooding. Major flooding happening in North Carolina that changes its shorelines.

Do You Want To Know?

The state of Louisiana is totally gone. It becomes a marshy swamp filled with pestilence. Mosquitos coming out of Louisiana carry disease. These mosquitos bring disease to the rest of the country.

Changes happening to the state of Oregon. I see major earthquakes and flooding. I see parts of Texas scorched and on fire. I also see parts of Arizona being scorched. The islands of Hawaii are changed. Major volcano eruptions cause havoc to the islands.

Every state will have upheavals to deal with. I see people moving inward away from the coasts.

There will be a complete overhaul of the government and justice system. I do not see the Republican or Democratic parties in the future. I see a new kind of government that works better for the people. There will be a younger woman president. She has a slimmer build with dark hair. After her, I see a much younger man coming in. The indigos are coming into full power.

The old can never come back again. This goes for organized religion, too. I see its structure being shaken to its core. It is stripped away of beliefs and stripped away of defenses so the people can evolve themselves. I do see spirituality coming in strong. There will be two or three major spirituality leaders to bring this about.

Technology is still America's number one commerce. As technology advances itself, I see more high tech airplanes, drones, and espionage capabilities. I see a new kind of material for airplanes. There is no longer metal but a fabric covering on them. Because of technology, there will be a total overhaul of the military. War as we know it will end. Cyber wars are featured in the future. Terrorism will subside because it will be much harder for the people to hide. They are caught easily through this new technology.

I see the oceans and the water turning toxic. Major chemical spills in the oceans kill many fish. These toxic fish wash up on all shores. The oceans are now poison. I see people scrambling as they try to figure out how to filter the water. They will filter the water. I do see people in the future not swimming in the oceans.

A future major problem for America is the gas lines. I see gas explosions happening all over the country. One right after another. The gas lines must be replaced and how the gas is administered must change. I feel if we do preventative measures now and update these gas lines, we can avoid this tragedy and loss of human life. Unfortunately, I do not see any action on this until the lines explode.

I see pestilence problems all across America. They cause havoc to crops.

There are new ways of living and new structures being built. I see communal living. The time of people living by themselves is coming to an end. I see a different kind of housing. They look dome like and they are totally energy efficient. America becomes the leader in solar energy living.

All schools are online. There will be a new kind of virtual reality. Students can use this virtual reality to visit places around the world without ever leaving their homes. In the future, I see virtual reality advancing where you will be able to not only see but feel and smell as well. This will open endless possibilities for education. Students will be taught quicker.

I see America and Mexico becoming friends. There will be new deals in place that will strengthen that friendship. There will be parts of Mexico scorched like I saw for Texas and Arizona. Mexico looks worse.

There will be new birds discovered in America. These birds come from the waterways.

I do not have a timeline when these predictions will happen. I am being shown that technology has speeded up the process.

I want to end this chapter with some positive things I saw. First of all, America is still strong and in the forefront. There is no more combat war because wars will be fought with drones and robot looking things. Eventually, there will be no more war of any kind.

Humanity continues to evolve in a positive direction. Eventually, the fast- paced life goes by the wayside. Humans will not need computers or phones. All information will be available to them. I found it surprising that as humanity advances, they go back to living off of the land. There is no more ego. I was thrilled to see the spiritual advancements they accomplish. No more fear-based thinking. These new American's truly know what freedom is.

CHAPTER SEVEN
PREDICTIONS: THE WORLD

The world is always changing. The only thing you can truly count on in life is change. Mother Earth changes as well. She allows us to live on her skin as we go through our human experience. We live on her but she does not live for us. She has a contract with God to let us be a part of her space.

We are parasites on her skin and she could wipe out the human race, plants, and animals very easily. She chooses to love us and she accommodates us the best she can. There are times she needs to breathe or stretch. She must stay in her gravitational pull properly and she will adjust herself when she needs to. This will bring on floods and other natural disasters for humans. We must deal with it and understand that we are her guests.

GERMANY

Corrupt from within, growing like a cancer. The government is stealing from the people. I see civil unrest and protests. I have a vision of the militia coming in with gas masks and shields. The militia is throwing gas at the protesters. The country's businesses and economy fails quickly. A major German official will be going to jail for corruption. A very young man comes in as the new leader. He straightens things out. The people that were protesting will rebuild Germany on a stronger foundation.

AUSTRALIA

The country of Australia becomes much hotter. There will be a lot of burning and fires. It will be almost inhabitable. A difficult place to live for there will be more disease and pestilence. The water is poisoned around the country and there is no more fishing industry. More and more sharks. Very dangerous waters. People do pull

Do You Want To Know?

together and adjust their lifestyles to stay in Australia. They will build highly technical dome-type homes that can survive the climate. Some people choose to live in the outback and they do suffer. They become native people even though they do not start out like native people. I see them living in mud-like huts. It is a split country. The population number will be half as much as it is now in 2019. It will survive but a difficult place to live.

AFRICA

There will be a new gem discovered in Africa. This gem is a very rare, highly sought after stone. It looks similar to a tanzanite because of its bluish purplish color. The people become very sick from a new disease. There will be a new leader that comes forward. He is a dark-skinned man. This leader is psychotic and poisons the waters to kill many people. Much genocide through this leader. Africa's light dims and dies out. The animals die, too.

FRANCE

Paris will never be the same again, I see its lights being dimmed. With that being said, I do see the French countryside blooming and flourishing. There will be an increase of tourism in the country parts of France. The vineyards will produce an even higher quality of wine which helps boost France's economy. There will be more bed and breakfasts established. Beautiful, quaint towns are featured. I see many ex-patriots from all over the world moving to the countryside.

ENGLAND

King George does take the throne. He is a very formal king that will be distant from the people. He does not want a queen but he must marry to produce an heir. There will be an arranged marriage for him. It will be a marriage in name only. He is distant from his child and the child's mother. Princess Charlotte, on the other hand, is a delight. She brings a lot of fun. She is very social and cares about people. She does remind me of Princess Diana in many ways. The people like her very much but they do not like her brother. The royal family does continue on. They are figure heads only. What the English government is now will change completely. I see the old government crumbling. I also see English newspapers and journals going out of business. There will be a new drug epidemic sweeping the country and killing many people. I see a terrorist attack and bombing on one of the royal palaces or houses. I keep getting a vision of King Henry VIII, so it could be a property associated with him. In the future, I see London becoming very crowded. It looks like India, with people living on top of one another. A major population problem in the city. There will be a huge memorial of Queen Elizabeth in a park. It will be very beautiful and a nice tribute to her.

HAITI/DOMINICAN REPUBLIC/CUBA

In the future, I see these three islands underwater. The water will be so polluted that many people will die from it. I do not see these islands in the future, they are gone.

SOUTH AMERICA

I see major earthquakes happening in South America that will change its landscape. Parts of South America gets so hot, I see scorching and burning. There will be a "hot wind" that blows through that will destroy many things. This "hot wind" will burn people as well. I see fields burning. The coasts of South America will be chewed up just like North America. There will be less land mass. The people do adapt but it is very rough terrain. I see a disease killing many donkeys and burros. The number one export of South America in 2019 will not be exported in the future.

CANADA

A prime minister or main leader of the country will be assassinated. This will be very unexpected. With this death, the country starts to change. Canada does not feel safe anymore. I see infrastructures crumbling as the economy tanks. The country gets much colder. I see poisoning in the lakes. I have a vision of many dead geese, birds, and fish washing up on the shores. The fish are not safe to eat. I see a population explosion happening. More and more people coming to Canada. The country will not know how to deal with all these people. There will be a movement in Canada to bring it back to what it once was. This movement will be futile. I do see Canada rebuilding its infrastructures but it will take many generations to do this.

RUSSIA

I see a lot of in fighting. Russia's government is going to change. The Kremlin is crumbling. This crumbling must happen in order for the new government to come in and rebuild for the people. There truly will be a Mother Russia as a woman becomes the leader. She will be the face of Russia. She will be a good person and helps this new society. Russia goes bankrupt and she helps rebuild the banking and financial industries. There will be more money around Russia because of its crops doing well. The people will be working together and building a better foundation. This woman leader is a great blessing for the country.

THE MIDDLE EAST

Death and destruction from terrorism. I see homeless women and children walking around starving. A majority of the population dies. There is desolation and darkness for quite some time. After this dark period, I see a pin of light. I see a new Middle East rising up. New people that do not know terrorism or war. These people are young and beautiful. All of the Middle East getting along with each other. They will be friends with the world.

Cheryl Lynn

ISRAEL

Israel has nuclear weapons which will help them with the major war I see in the Middle East. Israel stays strong and emerges the victor. Even as the Middle East turns dark, Israel keeps her head up and maintains herself. A new prosperous people living in peace. No more terrorism.

CHINA

The infrastructure of the country is weak and it crumbles. I see a failing economy that puts China in turmoil. The people rise up because they want something better. China will rebuild their finances and start helping the world. I see a big bank in China with much money flowing through it. Many financial institutions go through China as well. America and China become good friends. In the future, I see the country becoming very spiritual with miracle waters that heal. I see spiritual baths and healing fountains refreshing the human body. It becomes very beautiful as it opens its arms up out to the world.

JAPAN

I see Japan dark. Through natural occurrences, the country dies. Earthquakes and tsunamis are responsible for the death of Japan.

INDIA

There will be a disease in India that will take many lives. Terrorism within the country increases. I see India on fire as a hot wind destroys land and property. This fire wind scorches the people and animals. After this destruction, three strong leaders come forward. They rebuild the cities. A new crop for India brings in much money and the economy turns around. No more poverty. India becomes an economic force in the world. The country is strong and beautiful in the future.

Do You Want To Know?

NORTH/SOUTH KOREA

In the future, Korea dies of its own hand. The structure is weakened as the people become sick. This could be from poison from its leadership. Self-imploding. The people will try to save the country but in the long run it will not work. I see Korea desolate and uninhabitable. The Korean people will immigrate to other countries and survive.

CHAPTER EIGHT
GOD BLOCKERS

God is always present with you. Not a single moment of your creation are you void of God. You are part of the vast Universe and are able to access the unlimited power it provides. As God's child, you have every right to live your life's purpose in peace and happiness. It does not matter if you are on a different planet or earth. All are the same with God. Being human is difficult. You are bombarded by negativity constantly as fear and ego thrive on earth. No other spirit in the Universe has negativity, only humans. We are the least advanced because of this. The following issues can delay your blessings and it is up to you to resolve them. Once you remove these blockages in your life, it is a green light for God and the angels to move you forward.

EGO

The negative fear-based demon in your head. The liar that has you believing you are nothing, you deserve nothing. It loves to keep you in guilt and creating stress and anxiety in your life. It knows the Universal Law of "what you think and what you speak is what you will manifest". It knows to keep you in negative thinking and self- hate. It feeds on fear. It knows that worry and anxiety is fear of future events that have not happened yet in your life. And through the Universal Law, you will create those future negative events. The ego most certainly does not want you to be happy and in joy. And while you are in the lower energies with it, you will not. You must get out of the lower negative energies and rise up past the ego. You do this through Archangel Michael. Archangel Michael is huge warrior angel with a mighty sword that can cut away all negativity in your life and raise up your vibrations past the ego. You need to call upon him immediately with this prayer (or something similar)

"ARCHANGEL MICHAEL, I CALL UPON YOU NOW TO CUT AWAY ALL THE NEGATIVITY IN MY LIFE AND RAISE UP MY VIBRATION PAST MY EGO! RAISE ME UP WITH YOU AND THE ANGELS NOW! AND I GIVE YOU PERMISSION TO OVERRIDE MY FREE WILL FOR MY HIGHEST AND GREATEST GOOD! COME IN NOW AND MAKE THE MIRACLES HAPPEN!"

Once you do this, totally surrender everything to Archangel Michael. And remember, all negativity and negative thinking is from that devil the ego. God and the Universe is always loving and positive!

FREE WILL

Free will is complicated. On the one hand, it is a gift to us created by God that allows us to live our life on our terms. Our free will blocks interference from Archangels, Angels, Spirit Guides, Guardian Angels, Ascended Masters, Saints, our Higher Self, and even God from coming in to help. We must give them permission to override our free will for our highest and greatest good. Yes, even God does not cross the free will He created unless we ask Him to! You cannot change anybody's free will but your own. If you are trying to change or mold someone into who you think they should be, stop it right now and put the energy on yourself. We have the right to enforce our free will and take what life throws at us. For some people, that is their choice. However, those of you reading this book are asking for help in your lives. Many of you are stuck in negative cycles that never end. Release your free will to God for your highest and greatest good. Once you do that, then it is God's Timing, God's Interventions, God's Will. Have no perfectionism on how or when God helps. Just know He will and that His timing is perfect timing.

Cheryl Lynn

NOT TOTALLY SURRENDERING TO GOD

This ties into your free will. Once you totally surrender yourself to God, you must stay in the "NOW" and find your inner peace. This is where true faith comes in. God's plans and timing is different than yours. And please know that if other people's free will is involved in your blessings, it will take time. Humans are fearful of the unseen. Fear is humanities biggest problem. You must overcome fear in all forms in your life. There is nothing to fear. You are creating fear. The lower energies on earth thrive on fear. When you get into fear and doubt, this will block God. Remember that the Universe is always loving and positive. Put your faith and trust in that. Living in the positive. Call upon the angels for help if you feel yourself getting stuck in the lower negative energies. Call upon them, that is why they are here! Truly surrender yourself to God and unblock the river of blessings flowing your way.

YOUR NEGATIVITY TO YOURSELF AND OTHERS

It is true there is a duality present in everyone's lives. You must experience darkness to know the light. The negative energy is there just like the positive. As humans, we do experience negative things. Fear and darkness is stressful and scary. Demons and lower energies are on the earth.

This does not mean you give into the negativity. Just the opposite. You have the power to stay in the positive where your true spirit lives. You must distance yourself from people and situations that can bring down your energy. If you choose to dwell in the negative and lower energies, you block God. You manifest only negative. It is very important for you to stop all negative things you are doing to yourself and others. Clear away all the negative vices in your life like smoking, drinking, and drugs. Drink plenty of water and change your diet to the healthiest you can for yourself. If you are in an abusive relationship of any kind, it is time to leave. You cannot change the person's free will. Love yourself as God loves you and walk away. Be very careful about the music and entertainment you listen to. If it is based in low energy negativity, time to find more positive ones to spend your time.

Do You Want To Know?

If you are the cause of hurting another person or animal, stop this immediately! Give everything to God. Life is a journey. Time to make that journey a positive one.

CHAPTER NINE
MESSAGES FOR HUMANITY

I love being a psychic and lightworker. Every moment I am tapped into the spirits. I asked the Universe to come through for those of you reading this book. To give their messages directly to you without filter. I have channeled them and have written down exactly as they came through. Read for yourselves how much they love you!

GOD:

"It does not matter who you are, it does not matter what you do, I love you as you are. You will never be alone. The whole world will never be alone, I will be with you every second, every moment. There is not one moment that I have not been with you. Sometimes you do not recognize me but I am in everything. I am in everyone. And you are perfect. You are my child. You are my creation. And I love you as you. There has not been a moment in anyone's life where I had not been part of it and I will continue to be part of it. Times are changing and I am with all of you during this change. You are strong. You are all strong to move forward as these changes are made. And I am there at every moment. You are not alone. If you only knew the strength that you have through Me and through yourself, you would never fear again. Believe this, I do not judge you. I do not judge anything. If I judge anything, I would be judging myself. And I do not judge myself because I am love. That is what I am. That is the reason why I do what I do. We are all part of a big tapestry in heaven. As I am, as you are. There has not been one molecule that has not been accounted for. You are part and you are welcome. You are free to live your lives and to perfect yourselves. You are free to be your true selves. Do not hinder yourself with fear, do not. You are more powerful then you will ever realize. I love you. I love you. You will succeed and you will prosper. Have no doubt. For doubt can cause misfortune. I am not fear. I am not doubt. Give all your fears and doubts and misfortunes to Me. I shall take it to heaven and disperse it. I will take it. Give it to Me. Whatever it is, give it to Me. Whatever is bothering you, give it to Me.

Do You Want To Know?

There is nothing too small or too great. Give it to Me. With it, I will replace it with love. I will replace it with peace. You are to find your true self, that is your mission here on this earth. Those of you reading this book, find your true selves, your path, your truth. This book will give you instructions. This book will give you guidance and I will talk to you and speak to you through this book as well. I will speak to your heart and you will know in your heart that it is Me. You will have discernment, those of you that read this. All of you hear my voice, have no fear, have no ego. Move on, you are strong. And remember, I love you."

JESUS:

"It is almost time for everything to come together as was written in the bible but also in other texts. I am part of the glue that brings things together. That brings people together. And I will bring you together. I am not a religion, I am a feeling. But I also have action. I require those that love me to have action because we love. As I said in the bible, I do not bring peace I bring a sword. But this is the sword of truth I am talking about. I am opening up vessels within people, within their souls. They shall see, the scales will come off your eyes and you will see clearly. I am sending my healing light to many, many people as this world hurts. And as people come forward, as they gather strength, I will be with them. As they speak their truths, I will be with them. Have no fear, come out of the caves. Come out of your houses, come out of yourselves. The ones that are trapped. Put all of your energy on me and I will help you. For I am a healer and a teacher. I am here to heal and teach all of you. There is no distinction between people. I am here for all. My wife Mary is here for all as well. Together we come in strong, to help. And now you are seeing the voice of the voiceless coming forward. That is part of my work and that is part of my wife Mary's work as well. We come in and we love all of you very much. I am here again for action. I am here to move things forward, to unstick and unclog. To cut away with this mighty sword that I have, which we all have. The time is coming when humanity is going to advance itself. You will have the clarity that you need to advance yourself. I will be there leading the way. You do not have to look for me, for I have already come again. I am part of this earth, world. I am part of everyone. I have had many, many incarnations throughout my time here on earth. Points along the way and I am here now. In different forms, in different bodies. The spirit is the same. As always, I am a healer and a teacher. As you love me, love yourselves. Have no fear about me. I am there to help you. I am strong. There will be no more temptations. There will be no more illness. Give it to me, I am a healer. I can heal you. You just have to believe it and release it to me. Many people have seen me in many forms. Some people have recognized me, some people have not. That does not matter to me. I will continue on my journey. I will continue on my missions. I love all of you. It is now time for the sword to come out to cut away the negativity. To lead the way. I can hold your strength, so lean on me. And together, we move forward. Have strength."

MOTHER MARY:

"Oh, how I love the world. I send comfort unto the world and comfort unto the children. I am working more and more with the children. These new children that are here now. I work with Archangel Metatron to advance these new children. I have grace but I also have love. I am strong, I am strong with grace. I send comfort unto the comfortless. I feed the sick, I feed the hungry. I am on every street corner. Care more for your homeless. Care more for your children on the streets. Care more for your animals. Care more for the animals. For the mothers, do not push the fathers away. I can give you the voice to speak. I can give you the assertiveness that you need. I do this out of grace and out of love. I do this out of integrity. There is no religion attached to me. I am available for all of you. I love all of you so much. I am your mother. I am the mother to the motherless. I have miracle waters that you can drink. I have miracles happening at every moment, ask for your miracles. Light a white candle to me and ask for your miracles. I shall perform them unto you. I am strength through grace. That is what I am. I love all of you so very much. "

Do You Want To Know?

ARCHANGEL MICHAEL:

"The time is coming right now for strength. The time is coming right now for action. I am here. Have no fear, I am protection. I can help you raise up your vibration. I can help the world. I am coming in through many, many lightworkers. Many people reading this book are lightworkers. That is why you are attracted to this book. You are part of me. I am here to cut away all the negativity. To get rid of that that no longer serves your purpose. I am strong. I am a fighter. Ask for my protection and security and I shall give it. All you have to do is ask. It does not matter who you are. All you have to do is ask. I am very straight forward on many things. I will give you total clarity about what you need to do with your life and where you need to go. I can help you with that. When you hear your voice inside, that's me. It is very strong and very clear. It's me. I can help you get rid of your ego and fear. I can be the action that you need in your life to move your life forward. I am here for action. I am here because I love you. All you need to do is ask. You do not need to worship me. Just ask me and be grateful for when the miracles do happen. It is as simple as that."

ARCHANGEL RAPHAEL:

"The world is so sick right now. The world is so sick itself. It is time for the world to heal itself in all forms. Not only humanity but the world itself to send beautiful loving light unto other people. I am with all of you, at every moment in every day. Not only when you are sick but with those that are well. I walk with you every moment. All you have to do is ask. And yes, I do come in with a green light of healing but it is all forms of healing. Not only your physical bodies but I can heal your spiritual bodies. I can heal your minds. I can heal your souls so that you can raise up your vibrations. The world is sick right now but the world will get better. Things have to happen in order for the new to come in. I know there is so much fear out there. So much uncertainty. Give your fear and uncertainty to me. I will disperse it into heaven. I will take it away. There are things in the life that sometimes you do not understand. But you will have understanding once you get to the Other Side. Give me your grief. Give me your mourning. I work with other angels. I will send peace unto you. I am a great healer. I am a great physician. So are you. I work with you to heal yourselves and to heal others. I am here for eternity. I am here to help."

ARCHANGEL GABRIEL:

"You have to have more joy in your lives. A better balance in your work and play. Joy and fun and play is so important. No only to your soul development but to your human experience. There is lack of joy in life. Just being that child again. Living those dreams again and doing fun things. The laughter. I love laughter. I want to hear your laughter. Have fun, have joy. Laugh. Play. Yes, there are things that you need to do on this earth. We angels have so much joy, so much laughter. Sing, dance, and create. Be a part of everything. Be a part of everyone. Your laughter, your joy. The world needs that right now. I will carry your laughter and joy. It is time for you to have fun. It is time for you to start finding your joy. I can help you with that. There is so much meanness in the world. There is so much negativity in the world. You do not have to be a part of that. To raise up past that is through your joy and happiness. Your laughter. Doing things together. Doing things with others. Things that make your heart sing. Whether it is through your work or through other things. Joy is in many, many things. Do not hinder yourself or your creativity. Do not hinder yourself on your life's purposes. I will help you, just ask me, I will help you. With it, I will bring joy. I will bring happiness. Just ask me."

ARCHANGEL URIEL:

"I am the Archangel of Light. I bring light to those in darkness. I can shine my light even brighter and dark places will be exposed through my bright lantern of light. When light is shined on the darkness, the darkness will dissipate. I will take that darkness. I am shining the light within others as well. If you have lost your way, you can call upon me for I have the lantern that can light your path. All you have to do is ask me. I can take your pain away through my light. I will lead you out of the path of darkness and negativity. I will lead you on your path, ask me. There is a lot of pain in the world right now, a lot of pain. Some of you reading this book is in a lot of pain. I will shine my light on you, just ask for it. When I shine my light, you shine your light. Together our lights in this world will magnify humanity and raise up vibrations. I will shine my light, just ask for it."

ANGELS:

"There are so many of us. Humanity does not realize how many of us there are. We are truly an infinite number. We are truly chips from God. There are so many categories, all you have to do is ask for your own personal angels. We respond to your messages. We respond to your requests. But, you have to ask us. Have no fear about asking us. We are here, ask us. And then, listen to us. We will give you signs. We will work through others. There are so many angels. There are so many element spirits in the world. We love you all. We are here to help you. Yes, times are difficult right now but they will change. You will be able to see us. You will be able to see our lights. Some of us come to you right now in lights. Pink lights, purple lights, white lights and golden lights. There are so many realms of angels. There are so many of us. So ask us, there is nothing that we cannot do for you. Just ask us, that is why we are here."

CHAPTER TEN
FUTURE VISIONS

Here are some future visions I saw. Most likely those of you reading this book and myself will not experience this in our physical human bodies that we have now. However, we will enjoy it in our spirit forms and future lives. The future is beautiful.

HUMANITY

Humans are going to evolve quickly. They will become more like the galactic universe. Humanity has been so far behind, but now they are going to advance themselves. Human bodies change, they become much bigger. Humans will be able to communicate with each other without talking. They will not need so much food and water to survive, the body will adapt itself. Different kinds of plants. Humans do not eat meat anymore. Beings from other planets interacting with humanity. Humans will be able to transport themselves to other planets. Humanity goes back to the earth, living more natural. Their bodies adapt to the temperatures, no matter where they live. Humans will have the greatest of advancements and technologies, but live very simply. Dome kind of houses, communal living, harmony and peace. Many races, all skin colors. More brotherhood and unity. Male and female humanity will be equal and the same. One will not dominate the other. There will be counsels and leaders but no more governments or kings. There is no more war. Many of the animals that we know now will be extinct. New animals coming forward that will be a help to humanity. Humans and animals together without violence. Humans at a higher level, closer to God. Better communications to the Other Side. Angels are seen more clearly. Humans are advanced spiritually and hooked into their higher selves. God remains God. There is no more religion. Humanity together has a beautiful understanding of God. The human look changes. Very tall with big hands and big feet. Different body structure and digestive structure. Humans look more galactical. They are about peace and working with the world. Mother Earth is very happy with this new humanity. No more computers or technology because they will be beyond that. Humans come to understand that we are all equal in the eyes of God.

SPIRITUALITY

All humans are spiritual. No more organized religion. More interaction with the angels, archangels, earth angels, and ascended masters. Humans are at a higher level. God's love is very strong. So much spiritual advancement that we present humans do not understand. Very common to see these spiritual beings interacting with humans. No more death. When people want to leave the earth, they just step through the veil. No more violent deaths. Humanity so much happier. There will be spiritual leaders, spiritual centers, and lightworkers among the humans that will help with any questions they may have and help them communicate to the Other Side to get more information. Everyone is in one spirit.

EARTH'S DEATH

Mother Earth is going through so many changes. Mother Earth does love us and she supports us on our journey has humans. Mother Earth lives for herself first. She was here before us and she will be here after us. Humanity eventually moves on to other planets. Earth becomes earth again. All natural with no animals, or plants. I see rocks, fog and gas with some water. Uninhabitable. She is going to live many years passed humanity. Eventually, she will lose her gravitational pull and die. She flings out into the universe and burns up. This is multi-millions of years away. Humanity will advance itself right off the earth.

TIME TRAVEL

Humanity will eventually learn to time travel, this will become something very common. I see a universal highway that they can time travel on. This is no big deal for the advanced humanity. No more ego or fear in humans to stop the time travel. Humans will be able to see other realities. They can time travel back and observe themselves. There is no more cars, planes or boats. They use time travel to travel one place to another. When humanity crosses to the Other Side, they will use time travel. A thought and they are there. Other beings on other planets will use time travel as well, no more spaceships for them.

LIFE ON OTHER PLANETS

As humanity advances themselves, they come to realize that they are the "babies" of the universe. There has always been life on other planets. There are so many other realities out there. Other planets and solar systems. Multi trillions of life on other planets which are very advanced, they have been trying to help humanity all along. High vibrational, intergalactical connections. All life on other planets are different. They all look different. Humans will get along with them. Intergalatical leadership coming forward. Some aliens want to experience living on the earth and doing experiments with the earth. Doing research like taking dirt samples, etc. All planets will be open to everyone. There will be no fear. No more negativity on earth, so the aliens will feel comfortable coming in. There will be a God based society. God is the aliens God, too. Open acceptance.

OTHER REALITIES

Humanity will come to know that there are thousands of other realities going on at the same time. As they are living their life in one reality, there is a splintering off of a thousand realties from their reality with different scenarios happening. Humanity will come to know the miraculousness and expansion of the universe. Waves and waves of past, present, and future lives going throughout the universe at the same time.

I see fractures and fragments coming off of these thousand other realities. Humanity will be able to tap into those energies and observe themselves.

Do You Want To Know?

SICKNESS, AGING, AND DISEASES

In the future, there is no more sickness, aging, or diseases. The body will be able to adapt. There is no more aging as we know it. I feel younger humans. I do not feel old humans. At a certain point they stop growing, there is no more age or age numbers. When a human is ready to die, they zip out of the body and leave it. The body disintegrates quickly once they step out of it. Disease is totally gone. If humans feel out of alignment, they get their auras and chakras recharged by physicians to keep them at an optimal level. No more births. There are female and male humans but they do not merge together to bring forth babies. There are no more babies. The humans come in younger and then they advance to what looks like their thirties or their forties. They do not get any older than that.

MY MESSAGE TO HUMANITY

The most important thing is to love God. To really know who God is, our creator. To tap into that beautiful energy that is God. The true God. The God that is love. To have no more fear or negativity. That it all comes down to love. It doesn't matter how advanced you are or what you do. God is not of the bible and God is not some religion, God is our creator. God is with us always and in all ways. Every breath we take, every molecule God is there. We can all tap into that. Do not listen to the negativity. Concentrate on loving one another as God loves us. We have so much potential as humanity to come together and we will. In this new society that I see as we advance. It is time. It is time to stop the wars, the prejudices, to stop judging one another. Stop worrying about what you look like. Stop all the violence towards children, animals and one another. This is not of God. We must become the best that we possibly can become. To trust, surrender and release all to God. That God is real. There are billions of spirits out there ready to help you and to become a part of your life if you let them. No matter what you look like or what your life circumstances are, God loves you just the same. You are not less than anybody else in this world. The whole universe, you are not less. To love yourself as yourself. God sees you with love, He does not see you with judgements. See yourself with love. And know eventually you will discover this. I would like for all of you here on earth to discover this before you get to the Other Side. Please know that God is not a judging God. He is not negative at all. The only person that judges you is you. So, give yourself a break and see yourself as God sees you. I see many great things for humanity. I see many advancements happening. I see many wonderful things for the humans coming in the future. I am a part of this intergalactical universe. This big quilt where we all fit in and have a voice. Learn the miraculousness of God, learn the miraculousness of yourself. Please know that all will be well and that you are important. Everyone is important and a part of this world. You have the same potential, the same power, as the greatest of the great humans that every lived. You have that inside of you as God has provided this. Believe in God. Trust God. Trust yourself that you know the true way. I see many great things for humanity, everything is going to be fine. Those of you reading this please know when you get to the Other Side you will experience many things in different forms, bodies, times, fragments, and realities. Through it all, you see God's love because it stays the same and never changes. I love you all. Do not fear the future.

THE AUTHOR

CHERYL LYNN is a powerful Lightworker for God. She is also a Psychic, Futurist, and Spiritual Teacher. It is her life's purpose to bring light to others through this time of human spiritual evolution. She has thousands of clients that she gives readings for. She is known for her amazing psychic predictions on You Tube. She continues on with her life's work. She is blessed by her spiritual dream team on the Other Side. She is also blessed by her family. Her son Mike is her greatest joy. If you would like your own personal reading with Cheryl Lynn, go to her website WHITEROSE-PRODUCTIONS.COM for all the information. She is also available for book signings and spiritual teaching/speaking events.

CPSIA information can be obtained
at www.ICGtesting.com
Printed in the USA
BVHW031717090920
588496BV00001B/61